Daniel
Coumba

*Life in
Tudor Times*

Shakespeare
and the Theatre

Jane Shuter

First published in Great Britain by Heinemann Library
an imprint of Heinemann Publishers (Oxford) Ltd
Halley Court, Jordan Hill, Oxford OX2 8EJ

MADRID ATHENS PARIS
FLORENCE PRAGUE WARSAW
PORTSMOUTH NH CHICAGO SAO PAULO
SINGAPORE TOKYO MELBOURNE AUKLAND
IBADAN GABORONE JOHANNESBURG

Designed by Ron Kamen, Green Door Design, Basingstoke, Hampshire
Printed in Spain by Mateu Cromo Artes Graficas SA

99 98 97 96 95
10 9 8 7 6 5 4 3 2 1

ISBN 0 431 06748 1 [HB]

99 98 97 96 95
10 9 8 7 6 5 4 3 2 1

ISBN 0 431 06770 8 [PB]

British Library Cataloguing in Publication Data
Heinemann Our World Topic Books. - Life in Tudor Times. - Shakespeare and the Theatre
I. Shuter, Jane
792.0942

Acknowledgements
The Publishers would like to thank the following for permission to reproduce photographs:
Andrew Fulgoni: p. 7B
Auckland City Art Gallery, New Zealand: p. 5A, p. 6A
Bodleian Library: p. 28B
British Library: p. 14A, p. 27B
By permission of the Trustees of Dulwich Picture Gallery: p. 25C
Govenors of Dulwich College: p. 12A, p. 15D
Marquess of Bath: p. 17B
Mary Evans Picture Library: p. 21B
Museum of London: p. 7C
National Portrait Gallery: p. 13B
Pitkin Pictorials Ltd/Lord Derby: p. 26A
Pitkin Pictorials Ltd: p. 29C
The Masters and Fellows of Corpus Christi College, Cambridge: p. 23B
University Library, Utrecht, MS842, F132: p. 11B

Cover photograph © University Library, Utrecht, MS842, F132

Our thanks to Mike Mullett of the University of Lancaster for his comments in the preparation of
this book.

Every effort has been made to contact copyright holders of any material reproduced in this book.
Any omissions will be rectified in subsequent printings if notice is given to the Publisher.

Money
12 pence (d) in a shilling (s)
20 shillings (s) in a pound (£)

Contents

1 Travelling players

Today people go to watch **plays** in **theatres**. They have to travel to the theatre. The **audience** (the people watching the play) sit in a dark room and watch the **actors** on a brightly lit **stage**. The plays are on for many weeks. They often have complicated **sets** (scenery) and **props** (things like furniture and books). The audience has to be quiet and not to eat, drink or smoke during the play. Things were different in Shakespeare's time.

William Shakespeare was an actor and **playwright**. He lived during the reigns of Elizabeth I and James I. When he was born there were no theatres built for plays to be put on. The **players** travelled the country, performing plays in the **courtyards** of **inns**, or in any open space. By the time Shakespeare died there were some theatres in London, but not in any other parts of England.

What was a performance like?

The actors performed on a stage, but this was sometimes just made from wooden boards laid across some boxes, or even the back of their travelling cart. The audience could crowd around close to the stage. They could come and go when they wanted. They often called out during the performance. They smoked and talked to each other, even argued and fought. They ate and drank during performances. If they disliked the play or the actors they shouted, threw things, or simply left.

The plays

Travelling players could not have complicated sets or many props. They had to have sets that could be put up and taken down quickly, and that would fit in their carts. Sets and props had to take a lot of rough treatment. Players had to have as few **costumes** (the clothes they wore to act in) as possible, too.

So the players had to do a lot of the work that sets and props do today. The words of the play had to tell the audience where the players were. Characters often began their scenes by saying things like 'I am scared in this dark wood,' or 'What a fine castle this is.' The words also had to tell the audience about the person the actor was playing. So they said things like 'Here comes an ugly old man,' or 'What a lovely girl she is.'

Problems of travelling

Travelling players had to spend a lot of time getting from one place to the other. They seldom performed at the same place for more than a day or two. Travelling was not easy, especially in winter when roads were muddy and carts often got stuck.

Another problem was money. There was no way to make sure everyone paid to watch each performance. People went round the audience with a hat, but the audience could wander off at any time without paying.

Travelling players, painted by Peter Breugel in the sixteenth century. The stage, set, scenery and props are all very basic. The actors are probably wearing their ordinary clothes to perform. The picture is of a group of Dutch players, but English players would have looked and behaved in the same way.

2 London's first theatres

London was a big city, full of people who wanted to be entertained. The first buildings to be put up for entertainments were not built just for **plays**. People could watch plays, bull and bear **baiting**, acrobats and magicians on different days. The buildings were like the **courtyards** of **inns**. They had a central open space for the performance. This was surrounded by several rows of covered **galleries**, with seating around the outside walls. There was only one way in, so the **audience** could only see the entertainment if they paid to come in.

Who built the theatres?

The first **theatre** was the Red Lion, built in 1567. James Burbage, an **actor**, built another, the Theatre, in 1576. Philip Henslowe (who was already the **manager** of a **bear garden**) built the Rose theatre in 1587. Soon Burbage and Henslowe were rivals, trying to get popular actors or plays for their theatres. There were also some indoor theatres, called hall theatres, in the city. We know less about them, but we do know that Burbage built one, that they charged higher prices and that they were much smaller than the specially built theatres. They were not used much during Elizabeth I's reign.

Theatres did not always last very long. They were built with wood and thatch and were a fire risk. They were often put up in a hurry, and made with cheap wood. The managers usually spent more money on decorating theatres, to make them look good, than they did on making sure that the building would last.

Part of a sixteenth century engraving showing an early theatre. People think it is either the Theatre (built by Burbage in 1576) or the Curtain (built by Burbage in 1577).

Source B shows the excavations of the Rose theatre, London, in 1989. The circular concrete columns, which are grouped together, are part of a later building. But you can see the line of the galleries with a gap in it (at the front of the picture) for the door. You can also see part of the line of the raised stage. The model in Source C shows how it might have looked in 1592.

3 The Globe theatres

The first Globe

The Globe **theatre** was built by Richard Burbage in 1599, on the south side of the River Thames. Burbage built it using parts from one of his father's old theatres, the Theatre. The **lease** of the Theatre had run out. The landlord would only lease it to them again for much more money, which Burbage did not want to pay. His lease allowed him to take anything that belonged to him off the site – so he took the theatre! On the night of 28 December 1598, Burbage and some of the **company** met a master carpenter and his workers at the Theatre. They carefully took the Theatre apart and carried all the timber that was reusable across the river. They used it to build the Globe.

The first Globe burned down in 1613, during a performance of *Henry VIII*. A cannon was fired as part of the special effects. The burning wadding landed in the thatch, which caught alight. Because the theatre was made of timber and thatch it quickly burned out of control. Despite this, none of the **audience** were hurt. The company were not hurt either, despite desperate dashes into the building to rescue as many of their **costumes** and **props** as they could. The only casualty was a man whose **breeches** caught fire. Someone threw his beer over them to put the flames out.

Can you find the first Globe theatre? It is in this part of a map of London, made by John Norden in 1600. The theatre behind it, wrongly named the Stare, is the Rose.

Source A

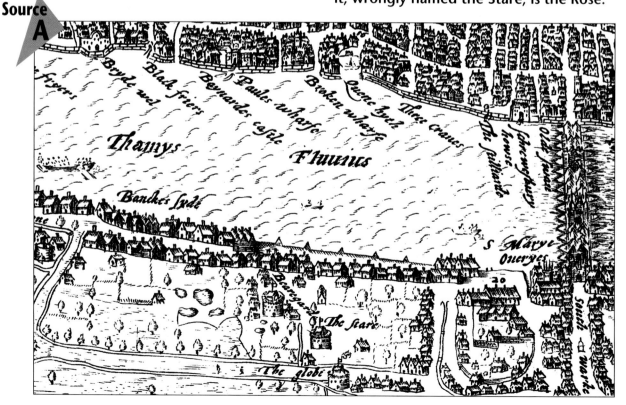

The second Globe

The second Globe theatre was built in 1614, on the **foundations** of the first one. Burbage and his **sharers** paid to have it built and decorated. It cost about £1,400. The Fortune theatre, built in 1600, had cost Philip Henslowe about £1,300.

The Globe had room for an audience of about 3,000 and gave them all the latest special effects. It had machinery to lower **actor**s down from the roof over the **stage**. It had a trapdoor in the stage, so actors could disappear below the stage, or rise out of the 'ground' at a dramatic moment. It had a curtained area at the back of the stage and a balcony above this area.

An engraving of London made by Wenceslas Holler in 1647. This shows the second Globe. It had been wrongly labelled 'Beere bayting'. The building labelled 'the Globe' is really the bear baiting house.

Source C

After dinner, at about 2 o'clock, I went with my friends across the river. In the straw-thatched theatre we saw the tragedy of *Julius Caesar* very pleasantly performed, with about fifteen characters. At the end of the play they danced together well and gracefully, as is the custom of the actors at the end of plays.

Written by the Swiss traveller Thomas Platter in 1599.

4 The stage

The picture on the right is the only one we have of a **stage** drawn at the time. It is a copy of a sketch drawn by a Dutch visitor to England in 1596.

The stage and the audience

The stage came right out into the **audience**. The people in the covered **galleries** (shown at the sides of the picture) had seats. The people in the open area around the stage stood up. These people, the **groundlings**, were very close to what was happening on stage.

The trapdoor

You cannot see the trapdoor on the stage, but you can see the space under the stage that the trapdoor led to. Some people say the drawing shows two big, dark posts holding up the stage. Others say the dark shapes are shadows and the light parts are curtains around it. In either case there is a space under the stage that the trapdoor led to.

Backstage

The doors at the back of the stage lead to the **dressing rooms** and to the balcony above. The balcony had several uses, depending on the **play**. Musicians played there. If the play needed a scene on a city wall or a balcony, the **actors** went up there. If the actors did not need it, seats in the balcony were sold for a high price.

The stage roof

The decorated pillars hold up a roof that often had some kind of sky painted on it. People could be lowered from the sky if the play had one of the gods appearing. The pillars themselves were useful for setting scenes. They could be pillars in a great house, part of a garden, or even trees in a wood. They were also useful for parts of plays where one person overhears things that other people say. The listening actor could hide behind the pillar and be seen by the audience, but not by the other actors. De Witt wrote a description of the Swan, which he said was the best **theatre** he visited.

Source A

There are four theatres which each show a different play each day. The largest and most magnificent is the Swan theatre. It has wooden columns that are painted in such excellent imitation of marble [an expensive stone] that you would believe that it is marble indeed.

Part of a description of the decoration of the Swan, written by Johannes de Witt in 1596.

A sketch of a performance at the Swan, made by Johannes de Witt in 1596. You can see the stage, the yard where the groundlings stood and the three galleries of covered seating.

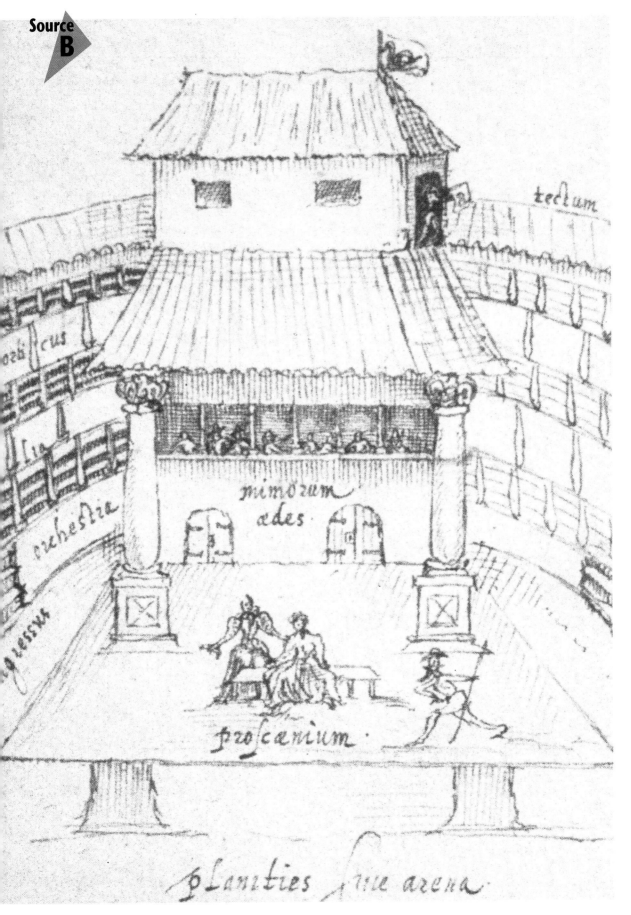

5 The audience

Going to the theatre

The **monarch** never went to public **theatres** in Shakespeare's time. **Courtiers** did not go often. They had **plays** performed privately. But other Londoners went to the theatre, from rich **merchants** to **apprentices**. They also went to other entertainments, like bear **baiting** and shows by acrobats and magicians.

When did they go?

Plays were performed between 2pm and 5pm. This was one reason why the **city council** disliked playhouses. **Gentlemen** could do as they liked, but if apprentices and other workers were at the theatre then they were not working, as they should have been.

What was on

There were several ways for **audiences** to find out when plays were being performed. They were usually put on at the same time each day. A trumpet was blown before the play began. A flag was flown from the top of the theatre when plays were going on. Handwritten advertisements were probably stuck up in various places. No adverts for plays have survived from the time, but an advert for bear baiting has. Play adverts were probably similar to this one.

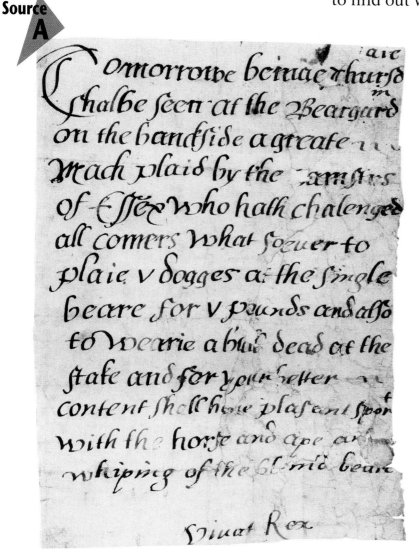

An advertisement from the time of James I for a bear baiting match, from Philip Henslowe's papers, which have survived from the time. The papers include his accounts and give detailed information about how theatres and his **bear garden** were run.

How much did it cost?

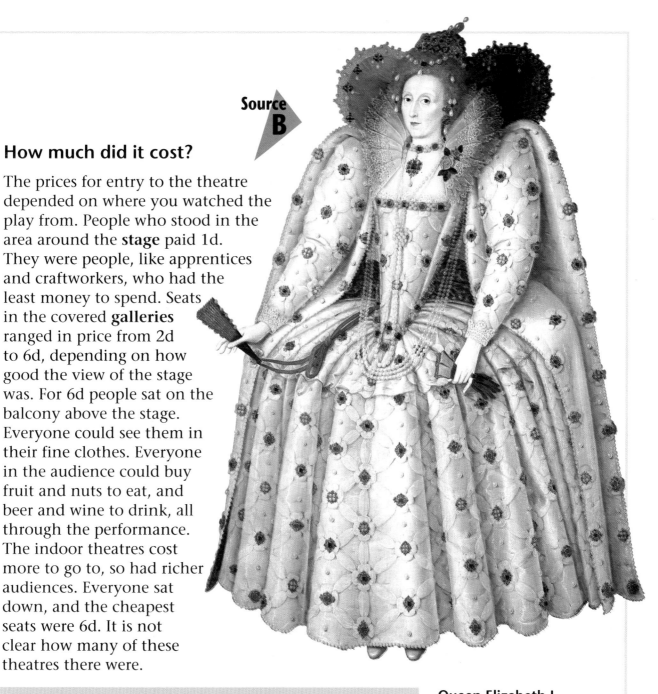

The prices for entry to the theatre depended on where you watched the play from. People who stood in the area around the **stage** paid 1d. They were people, like apprentices and craftworkers, who had the least money to spend. Seats in the covered **galleries** ranged in price from 2d to 6d, depending on how good the view of the stage was. For 6d people sat on the balcony above the stage. Everyone could see them in their fine clothes. Everyone in the audience could buy fruit and nuts to eat, and beer and wine to drink, all through the performance. The indoor theatres cost more to go to, so had richer audiences. Everyone sat down, and the cheapest seats were 6d. It is not clear how many of these theatres there were.

Queen Elizabeth I, painted in 1592. She loved plays, and often sent for actors to perform at **Court**.

Value for money?

The average craftworker earned 6 shillings a week (72d). He had to feed, house and dress himself and his family. Apprentices were only paid about 1d a week, but they had somewhere to live, and their food and clothes paid for, and had no families to support. Workers probably spent about 40d a week on food, more if they had big families. The price of food went up and up in Shakespeare's time. A large loaf of bread cost 1d in 1564 and 4d by 1616. Beer in the same period went up from $\frac{1}{2}$d to 1d. Beef went up from 3d to 5d for 500 g. The cost of standing in the theatre yard, 1d, did not go up.

6 The actors

Who became an actor?

Women were not allowed to act in the **theatre**. Boys played the women's parts in **plays**. The **actors** worked in **companies**. Some companies had a system of **apprenticeship**, like the craft **guilds**. Actors signed contracts to join the company in return for being taught their craft. They learnt by watching the important actors, and by playing the less important parts in plays. They gradually played more and more important parts. Some actors could act any part. But many of them became famous for playing a particular type of part, and had parts written to show off their skills. Sometimes **audiences** would boo them off the stage if they tried to play any other kind of part.

Getting a patron

The government had passed a law saying that companies had to have a **noble** as a **patron**. If they did not have one they would be punished.

Finding a theatre

As well as a patron, the actors needed a theatre to play in. They needed a **playwright**, too. The company bought plays from authors, but they needed someone who could write plays at short notice, or re-write a play that the audience had disliked. Actors were expected to be loyal to the company. The most important actors were often **sharers** in the company. They put money into the theatre and got a **share** of the takings.

Source A

Most companies had an actor who was famous for playing clown parts. This picture shows Richard Tarlton, one of the earliest clowns, who died in 1588.

Changing companies

Becoming sharers meant they were less likely to join another company or change theatres. Despite this, actors, or groups of them, did change companies from time to time and sometimes companies changed theatres. The managers, especially the richest of them, Burbage and Henslowe, were forever trying to get the best actors and playwrights for their theatres.

I understand that you have forbidden the company of players that call themselves mine to perform. I pray you, as they have my licence, to allow them to perform and give them all the help and assistance you can.

A letter, written by the Duke of Lennox in 1604. It is addressed to all mayors and JPs, who were local officials, so was probably carried by the players to show to anyone who tried to stop them performing.

Thomas Swinnerton and Martin Slaughter, two of the King's Men, have left the company. They have taken several copies of his Majesty's letter of patent for the company and have toured the country with a company of vagabonds, pretending that he is their patron.

A letter like Source B did not always mean the players had a patron. Letters could be misused. Source C comes from the papers of the Revels Office (who made sure players obeyed the law). This was written in 1616, when three groups of actors were prosecuted for using false letters.

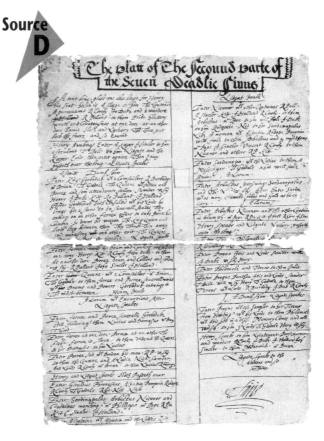

Actors had to perform a different play each day. This must have been very confusing. This is a 'running sheet' from the time. It gives a quick summary of the **plot** of the play and was hung in the dressing room. The title is The Plan of the second parte of the Seven Deadlie Sinns. The first part says: 'A text being plast [placed] on the stage for Henry the Sixt[h] being in it Asleepe.'

7 Costumes and props

How do we know?

It is not easy to find out about the **costumes** and **props** that were used in **theatres** in Shakespeare's time. Our only real record comes from written descriptions of some performances, descriptions of clothes and **scenes** in the **plays** themselves.

We also have the papers of Philip Henslowe, which have survived from the time. We know that theatre companies spent far more money on costumes and props than they did on the actual plays.

Court plays

The **Lord Chamberlain**, who was patron of Shakespeare's company, and who ran the entertainment of the **Court**, had his own collection of expensive clothes and props. These were looked after by the Revels Office, which kept everything clean and in good condition, and provided new things as required. Their collection of clothes and props was used by **courtiers** to put on their own plays, and were also lent out to any **company** that performed at Court.

Source A

Costumes

A rich cloak	£19
To get two cloaks out of pawn, one ash coloured velvet with gold embroidery the other long black velvet with silk lace	£12 10s
To buy fabric to make two women's gowns for 'The Two Angry Women of Abingdon'	£9
A doublet and hose of sea water satin	£3
A doublet and a man's gown of velvet	£6
A robe for Father Time	£2

Props

1 rock, 1 cage, 3 tombs, 2 coffins, 1 bedstead
2 steeples, 1 chime of bells
1 globe, 1 golden sceptre, 1 crown, 1 ghost's crown, 1 crown with a sun, 3 imperial crowns, 1 Pope's head-dress
3 clubs, 8 lances, 1 copper shield, 17 fencing swords
The city of Rome
1 golden fleece, 1 bay tree, 1 wooden canopy and 8 masks
1 cupid's bow, a cloth with the sun and moon on, 1 fork and garland for Neptune
2 mossy banks, 1 snake, 1 lion, 2 lion's heads, 1 lion's skin, 1 bear's skin

Some costumes and props that are listed in Philip Henslowe's account books and an inventory for the Rose theatre made by Henslowe in 1598.

Why were costumes important?

Some clothes and props were expensive. The 'rich cloak' in Source A cost Henslowe £19. At the same time a craftworker would be earning an average of £15 a year. But clothes were very important.

There were laws at this time that said what fabrics, furs and colours people could wear. Only courtiers could wear expensive fabrics like embroidered velvet and silk. So the clothes that the actors wore on stage told people about how important the character was.

The colour of clothes also sent a message to the audience. Black stood for evil, white for good. Yellow stood for a person in love. Clothes told you other things too. If an actor came on in riding boots, they had been travelling, people who were mad wore long-haired wigs with the hair flowing loose all around them.

A drawing made on a copy of Shakespeare's play, *Titus Andronicus*, showing actors in costumes. It is one of the very few pictures of actors in costumes that come from the time.

As well as clothes and props, actors needed wigs and makeup, especially to change boys into women. Luckily the light was not very good, so it was easier to fool the **audience** than it would be today. Afternoon daylight was usually all that lit the theatres. Performances to the **Court** were usually held in the evening by candlelight.

Not all props were expensive. A few pence at a butcher's shop would buy a stock of pigs' **bladders** filled with blood which, worn under the costume, made a realistic mess during fights and stabbings.

8 The plays

What can plays tell us?

Some of the **plays** that were performed in the **theatre** and at **Court** were also printed and sold. They are read, studied and still acted today. They tell us about the kinds of plays that people of the time enjoyed. They tell us other things about the time they were written. People have carefully studied the plays to find out how people in Shakespeare's time felt about things like parenthood, how to run the country, what makes a good king, witches, loyalty – almost anything you can think of.

Changing plays?

There were **speeches** in the plays that talked about issues of the time. The Revels Office had censors who read the plays and had speeches rewritten if they seemed to criticize the government. We must be careful not to treat the plays more seriously than people did at the time. The **actors** stuck to the **plot** of plays, but they often fiddled with the **script**. They left speeches out. They even put things in as they went along, especially in the comic scenes, if the **audience** was laughing a lot. **Playwrights** often complained that actors changed their words or demanded an extra speech or two at the last minute. We must remember that while plays can tell us about how people felt at the time, they were written as entertainment.

Choosing what to write about

The playwright seldom chose the subject of his plays. The **manager** of the company told him what they wanted. He had to please the actors by thinking about the people they could play and build the parts around that. He had to please the audience and write in lots of fights and special effects. He also had to please the manager by using all the special effects that the manager had built into the **stage**. These would include the trapdoor, the 'heavens' (which was worked by winding machinery), the pillars and the balcony level.

Source A

20.12.1597	Paid to Mr Dekker for additions to 'Dr Faustus' and 'Tamburlaine' [plays written by Christopher Marlowe] £1 5s
15.1.1598	To free Mr Chettle from the Marshalsea prison and lent money too £3
30.1.1598	Paid me by William Houghton, printer, for the use of Mr Dekker to write a book £1
1.2.1598	Lent to Thomas Nashe, while in the Fleet prison, writing 'Isle of Dogs' £1
4.2.1598	Lent to the company, to free Mr Dekker from the Counter prison £2

Some entries from Philip Henslowe's account books for 1598. Most of his actors and playwrights seem to have been almost permanently in debt to Henslowe. He treated them like his belongings, charging to lend Dekker to a printer to write him a book.

A typical stage with all the effects that a manager
would want a playwright to use in his plays.

9 A theatre owner: Philip Henslowe

We know very little about Philip Henslowe's early life, but we know a lot about his life as a **theatre** owner in London, because his account books and other papers from the time have survived. He moved to London with his master, Mr Woodward, in about 1570. Woodward died and Henslowe married Agnes, Woodward's widow. He was a hard-headed businessman. He was involved in lots of different schemes. He rented out his property, and bought and sold starch and goat skins. He lent money and ran a pawn shop. He charged high rents and was said to be hard on people who did not pay regularly.

Building the Rose theatre

Henslowe got involved in running theatres because he owned several **inns** in London where **plays** were performed. In 1586 Henslowe built the Rose theatre, in Southwark. Plays were performed there until 1601.

Henslowe saw the other theatre **owners** as rivals. He tried to get their most successful **playwrights** and **actors** to join his **company**, while trying to keep his own successful people. He tied them to him in as many ways as possible. He lent them money, so they were in **debt** to him. He flattered them and made sure they had good parts written for them. He even married his daughter to the most popular of his actors, Edward Alleyn, in 1592.

Source A

He made the company pay debts which their members have with him as private people.

He sold some **costumes** and kept the money.

He bought costumes which he said cost £60, which he charged the company. We had them valued and they were worth but £23.

He promised us £50 for keeping 1 day in 14 free so that he might use the theatre for bear **baiting**, yet he now says he will only pay £40.

The company spent £200 on plays, but get no copies.

The company have bought goods and plays for the use of the company which he keeps to himself and will not let us have.

He has given people that we hired as **apprentices** to other companies, which has broken up our company.

He has taken gold and silver lace from the costumes to use himself, and he has not paid us for it, or replaced it.

Some of the complaints made against Henslowe in 1615 by the company of actors. Even allowing for exaggeration he seems to have been a difficult man to do business with.

Why was the Fortune different?

In 1600 Henslowe and Alleyn built a new theatre, which they called the Fortune. The Fortune was big and square. Until then, theatres had all been built with lots of sides, to make their shape as close to a circle as possible. As they made money they bought more property and became more respectable.

In 1613 Henslowe opened a new theatre, to be used for many entertainments, called the Hope. But he spent less and less time running his entertainments himself. They had made him money, but he spent far more time in the last years of his life dealing in property. He died in 1616.

Henslowe ran various things as well as theatres. He ran several taverns and inns, like the one in this illustration from a book of songs printed at the time. He went to taverns too. His account books record several times when he spent 5s or so 'on good cheer in a tavern'.

10 A playwright: Christopher Marlowe

Christopher Marlowe was born in Canterbury in 1564. His father was a shoemaker, not a poor man but not a rich one either. Christopher was a clever boy who got a scholarship (worth £4 a year) to go to school in the city. It was a long day, starting at 6 o'clock in the morning and finishing at 7 o'clock in the evening. He did well, and, in 1580, got a scholarship to Cambridge University. This one paid all his fees and gave him 10d a week, plus a free room and money for his washing and a **barber**.

Marlowe becomes a spy

Marlowe got his degree in 1584, and started to study for another one. But he took time off to go to Rheims in France and so the University refused to give him the second degree. What happened next was very unusual. Marlowe complained to the **Privy Council** (the Queen's most important advisers). They insisted that he got his degree because he had 'done Her Majesty good service'. Marlowe had been an English spy when he had been in France. The University gave in and granted him the degree. Marlowe moved to London.

Marlowe spent the rest of his life in London, Holland and Canterbury. He made his living by writing **plays**, which were very popular. His most famous plays are *Edward II*, *Dr. Faustus* and *Tamburlaine*. Marlowe was often in trouble. He was arrested several times, in London and Canterbury, for starting fights.

Marlowe's death

In 1593 Marlowe also found himself in serious trouble about his religious ideas. It was a crime to speak against the Church of England. Not to believe in God was a greater crime. The Privy Council was told that Marlowe had said he did not believe in God at all and was writing a book to prove that God did not exist. They put out a **warrant** for his arrest for **heresy**. If he was found guilty he would be executed. But before Marlowe could be arrested he was stabbed to death in a fight in Deptford, near London. There is some mystery about his death. The man who killed him was also a spy. He was soon freed from prison and working for the government again.

Source A

Christopher Marlowe was, in truth, stabbed by a serving man in an argument over a woman. [*Written by Francis Meres, a friend of Marlowe, in 1598*]

In Deptford, a village near London, Marlowe was stabbed by a man called Ingraham in a fight over a dice game. [*Written by William Vaughan in 1600*]

Marlowe started a fight, on the streets of London and was stabbed. [*Written by Thomas Beard in 1597*]

Some stories told by London writers about Marlowe's death. They show that without television and newspapers telling the story, lots of rumours spread.

A painting which is said to be the playwright, Christopher Marlowe. We cannot be sure this is Marlowe. It was found in his Cambridge college and shows a man of the right age. The motto, on the left at the top, says 'that which nourishes me, destroys me'. This could well apply to Marlowe.

11 An actor: Edward Alleyn

Edward Alleyn was born in London. We know he was an **actor** by 1586, because his name is on a list of the Earl of Worcester's **players** in 1586, when he was twenty. He soon became famous, especially for playing the heroes of tragedies. In 1592 he married Joan Woodward, the step-daughter of the **theatre** owner Philip Henslowe. He acted with the Lord Admiral's Men, who played at Henslowe's theatre in London. He also went on **tour** most summers.

Plague

The summer tours happened if the theatres were closed by the **Privy Council** (which they were, regularly) or if there was plague in London. Plague was an infectious **disease** that broke out in the summer months. London was struck by the plague almost every year. If the plague struck, the theatres were shut down and the **company** went on tour, usually until the plague stopped.

Alleyn on tour

Alleyn exchanged letters with his wife and her family when he was away. These letters show us a different man from the businessman who helped Henslowe run theatres and **bear gardens**. In his letters he shows how much he cares for his wife, his house and his garden.

Back in London

When Alleyn was on tour he only had to worry about the company. When he was in London he had far more business to attend to. He and his father-in-law, Henslowe, were involved in running several theatres and a bear garden. They worked on the building of the Fortune theatre together.

While Henslowe had **shares** in the theatre, it was Alleyn who was expected to deal with day-to-day problems, from quarrelling actors to dishonest fee collectors. He acted in the theatres and even took part in the **baiting** of various animals, including a lion!

Source A

My dear sweet mouse,

I hope that you are all well and that, while the plague is all around you, it will leave your house alone. I advise you to keep the house clean and throw water out of the front and back doors each night. Also keep rue and herb of grace in your windows and pray to God. I have no news for you, but that we are all well. I have sent my white waistcoat home with the man who brings this letter, for it is too much trouble to pack. I wish you would dye my orange stockings black for winter wear, and send me news of my garden. Remember to plant spinach in the bed we were growing parsley in.

From a letter from Alleyn to his wife Joan, written in the summer of 1593. He was on tour during the plague.

Retirement

Alleyn's last recorded performance as an actor was in 1603. From then on he seems to have concentrated on renting out the property that he had bought and being a respectable businessman. In 1605, he bought the manor of Dulwich and other lands around it. He moved to Dulwich from Southwark and began to build Dulwich College – a school, a schoolhouse, a chapel and some almshouses. It is thanks to the college that his papers (and those of Philip Henslowe) survive today. He died in 1626, aged 60, leaving everything to his wife as they had no children.

Edward Alleyn, painted by an unknown artist in 1626. It was painted either just before his death, or just after, as a memorial.

Source B

Sir,

John Russell, who you employed to gather in the money is often false to us. We have warned him many times about helping himself from the box. He has vowed not to do so but we think he still does. So, for your sake, we have stopped him collecting the money and made him a stage helper. We will even pay him extra for mending the clothes. I hope you will approve of this, for it was done for your sake, Will Byrd.

From a letter written to Alleyn by the actor William Bird. The letter has no date, but must have been written between 1592 and 1603.

12 William Shakespeare 1

Shakespeare was born in Stratford on Avon in 1564. His father, John, was an important man in the town. Like many other townsmen, he owned property that he rented out. He sent William to grammar school. Stratford had regular visits from travelling **companies** during his boyhood. By the time he was sixteen William was expected to help his father with his business. In 1582 he married Anne Hathaway, a woman eight years older than he was. They moved in with his parents and soon had three children.

Shakespeare goes to London

Shakespeare did not stay in Stratford to help run his father's business. Some time after 1585 he went to London. By 1592 he was already a well-known **actor** and **playwright**. He joined an acting company, probably Lord Strange's Men. It was led by Richard Burbage, the actor.

Shakespeare would have started at the bottom in the company, as he had no money or experience to become one of the **sharers**. These were the most important actors who put money into the company and took a **share** of the earnings. It is likely that he began by taking small parts and rewriting **speeches** and parts for other people's plays.

Shakespeare's first plays

Among his first plays are those that tell the story of King Henry VI. They were very popular. In 1592, Henslowe (at the Rose) collected £3 16s 8d in entry money. This was the most collected in that season. A craftworker would have had to work for thirteen weeks to earn that amount of money. Other plays that year made from 17s to £2 10s.

Ferdinando Lord Strange, painted in the 1590s by an unknown artist. Lord Strange was the patron of the group of actors that Shakespeare probably joined when he first came to London.

Lord Strange's Men went on **tour** in the summer of 1592, with Edward Alleyn and some of the company from the Rose. The Rose had been closed because of some riots by **apprentices.** These were blamed on the theatre. Soon after the company left, the plague, an infectious **disease**, hit London.

The theatres did not re-open until the summer of 1594. Lord Strange's Men went on tour again with the Rose theatre company. We do not know if Shakespeare went with them, or stayed with another **patron** of his (the Earl of Southampton), or went home to Stratford. In 1594 he re-joined his old company. Lord Strange had died. They became the Lord Chamberlain's Men, playing at the Theatre.

The Workes of William Shakespeare, containing all his Comedies, Histories, and Tragedies: Truely set forth, according to their first ORIGINALL.

The Names of the Principall Actors in all these Playes.

William Shakespeare.	Samuel Gilburne.
Richard Burbadge.	Robert Armin.
John Hemmings.	William Ostler.
Augustine Phillips.	Nathan Field.
William Kempt.	John Underwood.
Thomas Poope.	Nicholas Tooley.
George Bryan.	William Ecclestone.
Henry Condell.	Joseph Taylor.
William Slye.	Robert Benfield.
Richard Cowly.	Robert Goughe.
John Lowine.	Richard Robinson.
Samuell Crosse.	Iohn Shancke.
Alexander Cooke.	Iohn Rice.

The title page of the first printing of all Shakespeare's plays. It lists Shakespeare as one of the actors.

Some of the main events in Shakespeare's life

April 1564	Born
November 1582	Married Anne Hathaway
1583	Daughter, Susanna, christened
1585	Twins, Hamnet and Judith born
1587	Shakespeare went to London
1588–93	Wrote his first seven plays
1593–5	Wrote six plays (during the time when the theatres were closed by the plague all through 1594)
1596	Hamnet died
1597	Began to buy land in and around Stratford
23 April 1616	Died

13 William Shakespeare 2

Growing more successful

From 1594 to 1611 Shakespeare lived in London and wrote **plays** for the Lord Chamberlain's Men. At the same time he bought property in Stratford, and went back from time to time. He had become a **sharer** in the Globe **theatre**, and so was making money at last. Like most people of his time he put his money into property and became more 'respectable'.

Retirement

Perhaps Shakespeare grew tired of the rivalry between his **company** and the others. The regular closing of the theatre because of plague may also have been a problem. Whatever the reason, he began to spend more time in Stratford and less in London. In 1611 he left his lodgings in London and spent most of his time in Stratford. He wrote two or three more plays. He died in 1616, aged 52.

A sixteenth century illustration of the story of Macbeth. Shakespeare re-used stories like this in many of his plays. Other playwrights did this too.

The witches from *Macbeth*:

1st Witch: When shall we three meet again? In thunder, lightning and in rain?
2nd Witch: When the hurley burley's done. When the battle's lost and won.
3rd Witch: That will be 'ere set of sun.

King Henry V, speaking to his men in battle:

Then imitate the action of the tiger;
Stiffen the sinews, summon up the blood,
Disguise fair nature with hard favoured rage ...
Cry, 'God for Harry! England and Saint George!'

Romeo from *Romeo and Juliet*:

But soft, what light through yonder window breaks?
It is the east, and Juliet the sun.
See how she leans her cheek upon her hand;
Oh that I were a glove upon that hand,
That I might touch that cheek.

Shakespeare wrote speeches that fitted the characters in the play. Not everyone speaks in the same kind of way. In the extracts above, the witches chant, even when not casting a spell. Henry V uses musical words and the image of a fierce beast to stir his men up to fight. The way Romeo speaks tells you that he is in love with Juliet.

IVDICIO PYLIVM GENIO SOCRATEM, ARTE MARONEM,
TERRA TEGIT, POPVLVS MÆRET, OLYMPVS HABET

STAY PASSENGER, WHY GOEST THOV BY SO FAST,
READ IF THOV CANST, WHOM ENVIOVS DEATH HATH PLAST
WITH IN THIS MONVMENT SHAKSPEARE: WITH WHOME,
QVICK NATVRE DIDE WHOSE NAME, DOTH DECK Y TOMBE,
FAR MORE, THEN COST: SIEH ALL, Y HE HATH WRITT,
LEAVES LIVING ART, BVT PAGE, TO SERVE HIS WITT.
OBIIT ANO DO 1616
ÆTATIS 53 DIE 23 AP.

Shakespeare's memorial in Trinity Church, Stratford on Avon.
It was done by a London monument carver, presumably at the
request of Shakespeare's family, soon after his death.

Glossary

actor a person who performs a play

audience the people who go to watch some kind of performance

apprentice a young boy who works for a master to learn a craft

baiting to set dogs on to bulls and bears to fight and kill them

barber a person who cuts hair

bear garden a place where baiting goes on

bladder the bag inside a person or animal that holds its urine

breeches short, puffed out trousers

city council the group of important townsmen who run the city

company the group of actors who all work at a theatre to put on a play

costume the clothes an actor wears when acting

Court the monarch and the people who live and work with him or her

courtier a person who lives and works with the monarch

courtyard the piece of ground in the middle of an inn

debt money owed to someone

disease sickness

dressing rooms the part behind the stage where the actors change into their costumes

foundations a solid base, usually dug into the ground, coming up to ground level, on which buildings are built

galleries The parts of the theatre that were covered and had seating built into them. There were usually three of them, one on top of the other.

gentleman a man with an income of between £500 and £700 a year

groundling a person who pays to stand in the space surrounding the stage to watch a play

guild A town organization which runs a craft. Everyone with that skill has to pay to join the guild, or they cannot work in the town.

heresy having ideas about religion that do not agree with the accepted religion of the country

inn A place where travellers could stop and eat, drink and sleep overnight. Inns were often built as a square, with an open courtyard in the middle.

lease an agreement allowing someone to use land that belongs to somebody else, for a fixed period of time, and for payment

Henry VII		Henry VIII
1485	1509	

Lord Chamberlain the man who ran the entertainment at Court for the monarch

manager The person who organized the running of theatres. Managers usually owned part of the theatre, but not always the whole of it.

merchant a person who buys and sells things

monarch a king or queen

noble A person from a rich and important family. Nobles had titles like 'lord' or 'Sir'.

patron A person who helps someone else. Patrons were more important than the person they were helping. They might help by asking for favours or a job from someone even more important.

play a story written to act out on the stage in front of an audience

players actors

playwright a person who writes plays

plot when talking about plays it means the story of the play

Privy Council the important men at Court whom the monarch chooses to advise him or her on how to run the country

props short for 'properties', stage equipment which can be carried around, anything from furniture to pieces of paper

scene a part of a play

script the words of a play, written out so actors can learn their words

set The part of the stage, with scenery and props that the audience can see

share in Shakespeare's time having a share in the theatre meant that you were given part of the money that was taken at each performance

sharer Someone with a share in the theatre. Sharers were usually the most important actors.

speech what an actor says in a play

stage The place the actors act on. Theatres had stages built. Travelling actors acted on whatever they could find, sometimes even the backs of carts.

theatre a place built especially for performing plays

tour To go around the country putting on plays at different towns and villages. Actors usually went on tour in the summer, when travel was easier.

vagrant a person who wandered around the country with no home, no work and no master.

warrant a written order to arrest someone

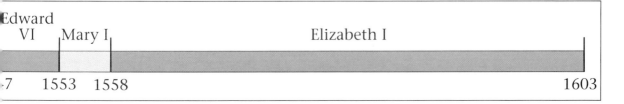

INDEX

Plain numbers (3) refer to the text. Bold numbers (**3**) refer to a source. Italic numbers (*3*) refer to a picture. Underlined numbers (<u>3</u>) refer to an information box.